FAMILY LAW AND PRACTICE

Divorce law and procedure

QUESTIONS AND SUGGESTED ANSWERS

Written by Steve J Norton
LLB, GDL, MA, MRES, LPC

Copyright © Stephen Norton 2019
All rights reserved.
ISBN-13: 9781704376370

The right of Stephen Norton to be identified as the author of this work has been asserted by him in accordance with the Copyright, Designs and Patents Act 1988.

All rights reserved. No part of this publication may be reproduced, stored in the retrieval system, or transmitted, in any form or by any means (electronic, mechanical, photocopying, recording or otherwise), without the prior written permission of the author.

Dedicated to Barbara and Leah

Acknowledgements

I have drawn on a number of sources in compiling the questions and answers for this book. I have used relevant LPC CLP guide on Family Law and Practice as a useful source on practical application. I have also used academic texts and exam guides as well as my own exam notes to compile questions for this series of guides that will be useful for those preparing for practice exams. In addition I drawn also on exam materials produced by the Chartered Institute of Legal Executives (CILEX) who produce extremely useful law and practice materials.

INTRODUCTION

I wrote this guide book as I found the subject of family law and practice very interesting when I studied it as an elective on the Legal Practice Course (LPC). I did not study this subject academically as I studied different electives in my undergraduate and post-graduate legal studies but having grown older and become a husband and a parent (slightly later in life), family law and practice seemed to become more relevant based on my own experiences. I hope those studying this area of law, and anyone else interested in how family law and practice applies in practical situations find the question and answer format useful. They are aimed at the practical application of family law rather than any attempt at academic discussion or analysis, for those starting legal practice courses. I have used a number of practical questions and suggested answers and included a few examination problem scenarios similar to those found on legal practice courses. I hope I have broken up the different elements into manageable chunks in shortish guides following the syllabus of legal practice courses. I have updated this guide to take account of the Divorce, Dissolution and Separation Act 2021 expected to become law by the end of this year.

I hope you find these guides useful for your studies or anyone else who may be interested in learning about some of the practical steps involved in different areas of family law. In this guide I deal with the subject area of divorce law and procedure.

CONTENTS

CHAPTER 1
Marriage – Outline of key concepts
General questions and suggested answers

CHAPTER 2
Divorce in outline
General questions and suggested answers

CHAPTER 3
Divorce procedure
General questions and suggested answers

CHAPTER 4
Problem scenarios
Questions and suggested answers

CHAPTER 5
Possible further reforms?
Discussion of possible changes in the future

Table of cases

Bellinger v Bellinger [2001] HL 10

Cleary v Cleary [1974] 1 WLR 73 (CA)

Corbett v Corbett [1970] 2 All ER 33

Gereis v Yacoub [1977] 1 FLR 854

Hyde v Hyde [1886] LR 1 P&D 130

Katz v Katz [1972] I W.L.R. 955;. 3 All E.R. 219

Livingstone-Stallard v Livingstone-Stallard [1974] 2 All ER 766, [1974] Fam 47

Pugh v Pugh [1951] 2 All E.R. 680

R v Jackson [1891] 1 QB 671, CA

Reneville v de Reneville [1948] 1 All ER 56, CA

Table of statutes/Regulations

Domicile and Matrimonial Proceedings Act 1973

Family Procedure Rules 2010

Gender Reassignment Act 2004

Magistrates Act 1929

Marriages Act 1994

Marriages (Prohibited Degrees of Relationship) Act 1986

Matrimonial Causes Act 1973

The Marriage (Same Sex Couples) Act 2013

Divorce, Dissolution and Separation Act 2021

CHAPTER 1

Marriage – Outline of key concepts

General questions and suggested answers

Question

What was the traditional view of a formal marriage?

Suggested answer

Marriage was defined as *"The voluntary union for life of one man and one woman to the exclusion of all others" Hyde v Hyde [1886]* [i].

Question

Has marriage been defined in other terms in any case law?

Suggested answer

In *Bellinger v Bellinger [2001]* [ii] Thorpe L.J suggested that marriage should be defined as *"a contract for which the parties elect but which is regulated by the state, both in its formation and its termination by divorce, because it affects status upon which depends a variety of entitlements, benefits and obligations"*.

Question

What are the requirements of a valid marriage?

Suggested answer

- Both parties must be over 16 (Age limit set by the <u>Magistrate's Act 1929</u>).

- Marriage not prohibited. The <u>Marriages (Prohibited Degrees of Relationship) Act 1986</u> lists marriages that are prohibited being against public policy. These would be those where there was a genetic risk to any children from the marriage due to their parents being too closely related. For instance a man cannot marry his mother, grandmother, sister, daughter or granddaughter. Similarly, a woman may not marry her father, son, brother, grandfather, grandson, etc. In terms of non-blood relationships this includes adopted children (but adopted siblings may marry if over 21).

- Bigamy. One or both of the parties are

already married.

- The statutory formalities have been correctly followed. There must be a formal ceremony (religious or civil) with at least two witnesses present. The marriage must have conducted by someone authorized. It must have taken place in a church, registry office or somewhere authorized by the Marriages Act 1994.
- It must be a voluntary union. The marriage must not have taken place under threat, whilst drunk or on drugs or by mistake.
- A man and a woman. Both are of the opposite gender. A sex-change operation does not change a person's gender where a `wife' was born a man *Corbett v Corbett [1970]* [iii]. Note: Under the Gender Reassignment Act 2004 (as amended by the Marriage (Same Sex Couples) Act 2013) now allows for a transgender person to *remain married* after changing their gender, provided their spouse agrees.

Legislation to allow same-sex marriage in England and Wales was passed by the Parliament of the United Kingdom in July 2013 and came into force on 13 March 2014, and the first same-sex marriages took place on 29 March 2014 (The Marriage (Same Sex Couples) Act 2013).

This only a allows a same-sex couple to marry in a civil ceremony. Religious organisations can opt out of these ceremonies if they object.

- The marriage must be consummated. Couple must have a sexual relationship after the ceremony.

Question

What are the formalities of marriage ceremonies?

Suggested answer

In a Church of England ceremony the couple marrying need to obtain one of the following:-

- Banns published announcing the marriage to be read out in the church of both parties on 3 Sundays during the three Sundays during the 3 month period of the wedding.
- Common License issued by the

Bishop. The parties need to swear that there is no legal impediment to prevent their wedding. One of the parties must reside in the parish for at least fifteen days prior to the wedding taking place.
- Special License issued by the Archbishop of Canterbury. This allows a wedding to take place at any time and any location.
- Superintendent Registrar's Certificate. This will give notice of the forthcoming wedding at the Registrar's office. Twenty-one day's notice is required and the records are available to the general public.
- The wedding must take place in a Church of England Church and must be performed by a priest between 8am-6pm, and two witnesses are required.

In a Civil Ceremony:-

- A Superintendent Registrar's Certificate;
- Wedding should take place at a

Registrar's Office/authorized building or home (hospital if either party is ill);
- Under the Marriage Act 1994 buildings like hotels can be authorized to conduct weddings.
- Must be conducted by a Registrar;
- Between 8am-6pm;
- Two witnesses required;
- Ceremony open to the public.

Question

What are some of the legal consequences of a marriage?

Suggested answer

There is a mutual obligation for each married party to maintain the other financially. There is a duty to cohabit (live together) in the matrimonial home (unless they agree to separate for extended periods of time). The law will not force one partner to live with the other against their will (*R v Jackson [1891]* [iv]).

Both parents have a legal duty to children to maintain them until they leave full time education (usually between 5-16 years of age. Parents must also protect their children from certain dangers such as alcohol, being abandoned or prostitution. To willfully neglect a child is a criminal offence.

The surviving spouse has a right to inherit all of the estate (or part of it) of their deceased spouse where there is no will (intestacy rules) subject to any rights of surviving relatives.

Question

What is a decree of nullity of marriage?

Suggested answer

A court can grant a decree of nullity of marriage which will declare the marriage null and void, which is different from termination of the marriage. A void marriage is a marriage that was never a marriage and a voidable marriage is a marriage that was valid until it is annulled by decree. The parties in this kind of marriage must obtain a decree to become single again.

There are four grounds of nullity under S.11 of the Matrimonial Causes Act 1973 (MCA 1973) :-

(a) That it was never a valid marriage under the Marriage Acts;
(b) That at the time of the marriage either party was already lawfully married;
(c) That the parties are not respectively male and female;
(d) Where there are polygamous marriages entered into outside of England and Wales, that either party was at the time of the marriage domiciled in England or Wales.

Question

What makes a marriage void?

Suggested answer

A basis of a void marriage was discussed in

de *Reneville v de Reneville [1948]*[v] where it was described as one which never came into existence, no matter how long the parties had lived together they would never get the status of man and wife.

There are grounds provided under the MCA 1973, S.11 for a marriage to be void.

Question

What are the grounds for void marriages?

Suggested answer

Section 11 of the MCA 1973 provides the grounds for a void marriage under S.11(a) that it fails to meet the provisions of the Marriage Acts in that in S.11(a) (i) the parties are within the prohibited degrees of the relationship. No one may marry a person they are related by blood or marriage within the prohibited degrees set out in the Marriage Acts. The Marriage (Prohibited Degrees of Relationship) Act 1986 and Gender Reassignment Act 2004 lists all those who may not marry. This includes those blood relatives and relationships of affinity such as:-

- Father/Daughter
- Mother/Son
- Niece/Uncle
- Nephew/Aunt
- Brother/Sister
- Grandparent/Grandchild
- Half-siblings
- Adopted child/Adoptive parent

In S.11(a) (ii) either party in under the age of 16 (*Pugh v Pugh [1951]*[vi])

In S.11(a) (iii) the parties have intermarried in disregard to certain requirements as to the formation of marriage. In *Gereis v Yacoub [1977]* a [vii]ceremony at a Coptic Orthodox Church which was not properly licensed to carry out a marriage ceremony, so the marriage was void.

S.11(b) that a marriage is void if either party was already married or in a civil partnership.

S.11(c) that the parties are not respectively

male and female. Same-sex marriages are not allowed in English law.

S.11(d) Polygamous marriage entered into outside of England and Wales and either party was domiciled in England and Wales at the time.

Question

What is a voidable marriage?

Suggested answer

A voidable marriage is one that is flawed in its validity but continues to exist.

Question

What are the grounds that are used to determine if a marriage is a voidable marriage?

Suggested answer

Section 12 of the MCA 1973 sets out the 6

grounds available to declare a marriage voidable. There are:-

(a) Non-consummation of marriage due to the incapacity of either of the parties;

(b) Non-consummation due to the willful refusal of the respondent;

(c) Lack of valid consent to the marriage by either party;

(d) That either party was suffering from a mental disorder;

(e) That the respondent was suffering from VD at the time of the marriage in a communicable form;

(f) That the respondent was pregnant by another person other than the petitioner at the time of the marriage;

CHAPTER 2

Divorce in outline

General questions and suggested answers

Question

When can a party file for divorce?

Suggested answer

A party (the Petitioner) can only petition for divorce after <u>one year</u> of marriage.

Question

What is the ground for divorce?

Suggested answer

The only ground for divorce under S.1(1) of the <u>MCA 1973</u> which that the marriage has 'irretrievably broken down' . To show there has been an irretrievable breakdown, the petitioner must establish one of the **5 facts** below:-

1. Adultery - One party has had sexual intercourse outside of the marriage and it is unbearable for the other party to carry on with the marriage.
2. Desertion - One party leaves the other

and stays away for at least 2 years. The couple must live in separate households (even if in the same house). Party deserting must have the intention to desert. It must be against the wishes of the other party. There must be no just cause such as violence causing the deserting party to leave.

3. Unreasonable behaviour - The test for unreasonable behaviour was established by Mr Justice Dunn in the 1974 case *Livingstone-Stallard v Livingstone-Stallard* [1974] [viii] :-
"Would any right thinking person come to the conclusion that this husband has behaved in such a way that this wife cannot reasonably be expected to live with him, taking into account the whole of the circumstances and the character and personalities of the parties?"

4. Two years separation with consent – Both parties agree to live apart in separate households from the time they started living apart, or the date both decided their marriage was over.

5. Five years separation without consent – Where it can be proven that the separation has lasted at least 5 years

immediately preceding the presentation of the petition, then no consent is needed from the other party to divorce.

Question

Which courts hear divorce cases?

Suggested answer

County courts hear uncontested divorce cases.

The Family Division of the High Court hears contested divorce cases.

Question

Which are the two stages in a divorce?

Suggested answer

<u>Decree nisi</u> – granted after the divorce hearings are completed. The judge has

agreed to grant the divorce petition but the marriage is not yet over.

Decree absolute – Granted 6 weeks after the decree nisi if the Petitioner applies for the formal marriage certificate of divorce. If the Petitioner does not apply for the decree nisi within 2 years or the time limit will lapse and the Petitioner will then have to reapply to the court.

CHAPTER 3

Divorce procedure

General questions and suggested answers

Question

What is the procedure for divorce?

Suggested answer

(Undefended divorce: procedure checklist)

Petitioner

(1) Files at divorce centre:
(a) Marriage certificate;
(b) Petition + copy(ies);
(c) Statement of reconciliation (only if solicitor on court record);
(d) Fee or application for exemption.
(2) Receives notification of case number allocated.

Respondent

(3) Receives from divorce centre:
(a) Copy petition;
(b) Notice of Proceedings;
(c) Acknowledgement of Service.
(4) Returns completed Acknowledgement of Service.

Petitioner

(5) Receives photocopy of completed Acknowledgement of Service.
(6) Files:
(a) Application for decree nisi;
(b) Statement in support of petition.

Respondent

(7) *Both* parties receive a notice of the date fixed for pronouncement of decree nisi.
(8) Decree nisi pronounced.
(9) *Both* parties would be notified of any directions, eg further information or appointment at court
(10) *Both* parties receive copy of decree nisi.

Petitioner

(11) Petitioner files notice for decree nisi to be made absolute (after 6 weeks from grant of decree nisi) and the fee (if appropriate).

Respondent

(12) *Both* parties receive copy decree absolute.

A petitioner can now apply on-line for divorce.[ix]

Question

What additional documents need to be filed with the divorce petition and what are they for?

Suggested answer

- Marriage certificate (or certified copy obtained on payment of a small fee from the Superintendent Register of Marriages for the district where the marriage took place, or General Register Office.
- Statement of reconciliation – If the solicitor is acting for the client there is an obligation to file a statement of reconciliation which states whether or not the solicitor has discussed with the petitioner the possibility of a reconciliation and given him details of agencies experienced in giving him help

promote reconciliation (<u>Family Procedure Rules 2010</u> (FPR, R 7.6).
- <u>Fee</u> – the fee payable on filing the petition or remission form for full or part remission.

Question

What is the jurisdiction of the English courts to hear divorce suits?

Suggested answer

Jurisdiction is governed by S 5 of the <u>Domicile and Matrimonial Proceedings Act 1973</u> which incorporates Council Regulation (EC) No 2201/2003 known as Brussels 11a (See end notes for link to discussed of this Regulation in relation to the possible effect of Brexit[x]).

The English courts have jurisdiction to hear a divorce suit only where:

(a) Both parties are habitually resident in England and Wales; or

(b) Both parties were last habitually resident in England and Wales, and one of them still resides there; or

(c) The respondent is habitually resident in England and Wales; or

(d) The petitioner is habitually resident in England and Wales and has lived there for at least a year immediately before the petition is filed; or

(e) The petitioner is domiciled in England and Wales and has been residing in England and Wales for at least six months immediately before the petition is filed; or

(f) Both parties are domiciled in England and Wales; or

(g) If none of (a)–(f) above applies and no court of another EU State has jurisdiction, (see end note ix) either of the parties is domiciled in England and Wales on the date when the proceedings are begun.

Question

What is meant by `habitual residence?

Suggested answer

Some key elements under the context of Brussels 11a –
- A person can only be resident in one place at any given time
- Important to establish the `centre of interests' of a person's life (the centre of interests does not have to be permanent, only habitual, but must be stable in character - This might be done by evidencing a job, home address, GP, membership of clubs etc in a particular area)

Question

What is meant by domicile?

Suggested answer

A person acquires domicile in a number of ways:-

(i) Domicile of origin

A person acquires domicile of origin at birth. A child whose parents are married will benefit from his father's domicile. If his/her parents are not married it will be the mother's domicile. Where the child was born will be irrelevant.

(ii) Domicile of choice

Persons aged 16 or over may acquire a domicile of choice which requires firstly, residence in a country other than the domicile of origin and secondly, an intention to remain there permanently or indefinitely. This could be through a number of factors, becoming a citizen of that country, by purchase of a home or by length of time spent in that country.

Question

What are the various ways to serve the petition and other relevant documents?

Suggested answer

The petition must be served along with other relevant documents on the respondent and any co-respondent (FPR 2010, R 7.8). The following are various methods:-

- Service of the petition is sent by the via 1st class post by the court to the address given in the petition (usual method). The court attaches a Notice of Proceedings explaining to the respondent the divorce procedure with instructions on completing and returning the Acknowledgment of Service. Also sent is the Acknowledgment of Service which is useful as proof of service of the petition, and whether the R intends to defend.

- Personal service is service through the petitioner and carried out by them. A process server will be instructed, or the petitioner's solicitors will themselves serve the documents (the petitioner themselves cannot serve the documents on the R (FPR 2010, R 6.5 (3)). A certificate of service will be proof of service by the person serving the documents.

- <u>By court bailiff.</u> The petitioner may request bailiff service by lodging the appropriate form (FPR 2010 R 6.9). A fee is payable (unless the petitioner has sign a remission form). Any request for bailiff service must be sent with evidence that postal service has failed, or why it is not appropriate. A description of the R, usually a photo, must be lodged to help the bailiff identify the R. The bailiff will then serve the documents personally and file a certificate of service. Either the return of the Acknowledgment of Service returned by the R, or if not returned, the bailiff's certificate will be proof of service. It is unusual for a request for bailiff service to be granted if the petitioner is legally represented, as he/she will usually use a process server rather than bailiff.

- <u>Deemed service</u> is where the R does not return the Acknowledgment of Service to the court and the petitioner can then apply for deemed service if he can satisfy the court that the R has received the petition (FPR 2010, R 6.16). This is achieved by making an application without notice, supported by evidence showing why in P thinks the R has received the petition. He may argue her/himself that the R read the petitioner and then threw it away or an open letter from the R's solicitors referring to the petition.

- Service by alternative means may be used where efforts have been made using all other methods to serve the petition (post/personal) – FPR 2010, PD 6A para 6.2). If the order is granted, it will specify the alternative method to be used, examples are through advertisement in a local newspaper the R may read or on a friend or relative of the R he visits regularly, or someone he lives or works with.

- A last resort could be dispensing with service if all other methods have failed and the district judge is of the opinion that it is impracticable to serve the petition (FPR 2010, R 6.20). An application without notice should be made to the court setting out the grounds for the application (i.e. the problem locating the R). The P must show every effort has been made to trace the R to dispense with other methods of service.

Question

Are there alternatives to divorce for the parties?

Suggested answer

(i) <u>Nullity</u> can declare a marriage <u>void</u> at the outset as if it never existed for instance where the parties are too closely related to each other, or one or both parties are under 16 at the time of the marriage, or either party was already lawfully married (<u>MCA 1973</u>, S 11). A void marriage being one that never existed does not need a decree to end it, but as a decree is needed if financial orders are required, a decree is usually obtained.

A marriage will be <u>voidable</u> in certain situations such as: non-consummation for whatever reason; lack of consent maybe due to duress; an interim gender recognition certificate was issued to the respondent after the marriage. A voidable marriage will exist until such time as a decree of nullity is obtained.

As a general rule the petitioner must apply for the decree <u>within 3 years of the date of the marriage.</u>

   (ii) <u>Judicial separation</u>

An alternative to a decree of divorce is a decree of judicial separation (JR) (or separation order for civil partners). This will not dissolve the marriage but can be used for instance where religious beliefs forbid divorce.

The grounds for obtaining a decree of JR are the same facts that need to be proved to obtain a divorce (<u>MCA 1973</u>, S 1(2)).

The effect of the JR is that once the decree is obtained the parties are still married as the decree does not dissolve the marriage, it only releases the parties from the duty to live together. Existing wills will not be affected and clients need to be made aware that if subsequently a spouse dies intestate, his or her property will devolve as if the spouse was already dead, so the surviving spouse will not benefit, so they may be advised to review their will/s.

Question

You have been asked by your supervisor to draft a comprehensive guide for the firm on divorce procedure describing timescales and relevant court forms?

Suggested answer

DIVORCE PROCEDURE AFTER ONE YEAR OF MARRIAGE

Step 1 - Either spouse can apply for a divorce petition and this person is known as the petitioner. To do this Form D8 (divorce petition) and Form D8A (statement of arrangements for the children) if applicable, must be sent to the court together with the marriage certificate. The court fee for issuing the divorce is £550 (2019).

GROUNDS FOR DIVORCE

Step 2 - For the petitioner to be successful, he or she must show that the marriage has irretrievably broken down by establishing one of the following five facts as proof:

- Adultery of the other spouse;

- Unreasonable behaviour of the other spouse;

- Desertion by the other spouse after two years;

- Separation with consent after two years;

- Separation without consent after five years.

Step 3 - After a few days of the court receiving the petition, it will send the petitioner Form D9H (notice of issue of petition) confirming receipt of the petition and also when this was sent to the respondent. The court sends a copy of the petition and statement of arrangements to the other spouse, known as the respondent.

If the respondent has instructed a family lawyer to act on his or her behalf, then these documents will be sent to them. Where the reason for the divorce is adultery, a copy of the petition must be sent to this person. This person is known as the co-respondent, however, their name does not have to appear on the petition.

RESPONDENT REQUIREMENTS

Step 4 - Within 8 days (including the day of receipt) of the petition and statement of arrangements from the court, the respondent must send to the court Form D10 (acknowledgement of service). The respondent must state on the form if he or she intends to defend the petition, if there are any claims for costs are disputed and if there is agreement between the parties regarding the arrangements for the children.

step 5 - If the respondent intends to defend the divorce, within 29 days (including the day of receipt) of the petition and statement of arrangements from the Court, he or she must send to the Court a defence known as an 'Answer'. A defended divorce leading to a final contested hearing is unusual as the majority of parties reach an agreement during divorce proceedings. A defended divorce leading to a final hearing is also very expensive and public and can be reported through the press.

Step 6 - If you know the respondent intends to defend the case but does not respond within 29 days, you can apply for directions for trial. The petitioner must complete Form D84 (application for directions for trial) and Form D80 (affidavit of evidence) which are provided free from a court office. There are different versions of Form D80 for each of the five grounds for divorce.

RESPONDENT FAILS TO RESPOND

Step 7 - If the respondent or any co-respondent fails to return Form D10 (acknowledgement of service) to the court, then 8 days after the petition was sent the petitioner must get 2 copies from the court of Form D89 (request for bailiff service). With this form the petitioner must also send a photograph or a written description of the respondent or co-respondent together with a fee for each person being served.

APPLY FOR A DECREE NISI

Step 8 - If the divorce is not defended, then a few days after receiving the Form D10 (acknowledgement of service), the petitioner can apply to the court for the decree nisi. The petitioner must provide a sworn affidavit in Form D80 to confirm that the contents of the Form D10 (acknowledgement of service) are correct. This includes the following:

- that the respondent and any co-respondent has received the divorce petition;

- that the respondent and any co-respondent have admitted to committing adultery if this was the grounds for divorce;

- that the respondent consents to a divorce if the grounds for divorce were that you have been separated for and living apart for two years;

- that the respondent has agreed with the

- arrangements for the children.

- The petitioner must swear the affidavit before

- an officer of the county court or the Principal

- Registry or a solicitor and then send this together with the decree nisi to the court.

Step 9 - Once the court receives the application for the degree nisi, a Judge will review the paperwork to ensure that it is in order. If this is so the court will send both the petitioner and the respondent Form D84A (certificate of entitlement to a decree) informing of the time and date the Judge will grant a decree nisi. If there are no children, Form D84B (notice of satisfaction with the arrangements for the children) will also be sent with Form D84A confirming that there are no children.

The court then makes an appointment for the pronouncement, this being about 5 weeks after sending the application for a decree nisi to the court. It is not a requirement that the parties be present when the decree nisi is pronounced and the court will send to the petitioner, respondent and co-respondent Form D29 (decree nisi).

APPLY FOR A DECREE ABSOLUTE

Step 10 - When the decree nisi is granted, 6 weeks and 1 day later the petitioner can apply for the final decree called the decree absolute and submit Form D36 (notice of application for decree nisi to be made absolute). This is processed within a few days and the Court can then grant the decree absolute making the divorce final. The court will sent to the petitioner and respondent Form D37 (decree absolute).

Step 11 - If the petitioner does not apply for a decree absolute, then the respondent can apply 3 months after the date the petitioner could have applied for the decree absolute. This is 4½ months and 1 day after the decree nisi is granted. The petitioner can prevent the respondent from doing this if the petitioner can show that by doing so would create financial difficulties, where a final financial order for ancillary relief has not been granted.

Question

What is the prescribed form for a divorce petition?

Suggested answer

The divorce must be set out in the divorce petition (D8) following prescribed format (R.5.1 FPR 2010).

(i) Names of the parties and date and place they married (as per marriage certificate).
(ii) Last address where they lived as husband and wife.
(iii) Current occupations of parties and residence (provisions allow address of petitioner to be hidden where there is fear of violence from the respondent).
(iv) Information about any other court proceedings taking place in England or Wales (or elsewhere) that relates to the marriage or children of the family, or any

property of either person. Full details must be disclosed of any earlier proceedings, any orders made and when.

(v) Whether there has been any agreement between the parties or is proposed, regarding the support of any child of the family. This is only needed in relation to a petition based on Fact E (5 years separation), where grave the financial hardship defence may be relevant. The court needs to know about any existing arrangements or proposals.

(vi) A statement that the petitioner is applying for a divorce on the ground that the marriage has irretrievably broken down.

(vii) A Statement of Fact describing which fact under S.1(2) of the MCA 1973 the petitioner is relying upon. Along with this should be a Statement of Case giving details of the incidents the petitioner is relying on (but not the evidence needed to prove this). [xi]

(viii) The petition must end with a Prayer (Summary of what is being applied for) and the Statement of Truth). Basically this is the claim for any financial relief needed. It is important that the petitioner makes an application for all forms of financial order which could be required in the petition. Leave of the court will be required for a

(ix) later application if the petitioner fails to do this.[xii]
(ix) There is a section on claiming costs. It is not usual to ask for costs in divorce cases. Costs may be able to be claimed in some cases such as where the petitioner is paying privately in fault-based divorce cases. The costs set out in the prayer will only cover those costs that are incurred in dissolving the marriage. Any costs for financial orders can be sought in separate financial proceedings.
(x) There is a space on the prescribed form to add the date of birth of any child of the family and tick boxes to show whether the child is one of both parties, and is in education, training or work (this section is optional to complete).
(xi) The form is signed by the petitioner (and details of any solicitor acting).

Question

What are the changes expected under the Divorce, Dissolution and Separation Act 2021?

Suggested answer

The long awaited Divorce, Dissolution and Separation Act 2021 has passed through both Houses of Parliament and expected to become law before the end of 2021. This followed the case of *Owen v Owen [2018]* [xiii] where a husband contested a petition divorce and the Supreme Court ruled the marriage should continue until the 5-year period was exhausted (under the 5-year rule). They were not persuaded by his wife's strength of evidence of unreasonable behaviour and found it did not meet the test in s.1(2)(b) MCA 1973. The unease of the judiciary in reaching this decision when looking at changing social norms and the law in this area, led to the view it may be time Parliament looked again at this area with a view to changing the law.
The legislation in this case is mentioned above and the expected changes when the Act becomes law are:-

- When applying for a Divorce there will not be the need to attribute blame on the other party or come after a period of separation of at least two years.

- One or both parties can apply for a 'Divorce Order'. If both parties make the application, both parties must see the process through to the end.

- There will be changes to the terminology:
    - ✓ The Petitioner will become the **Applicant** (or Applicants)
    - ✓ The Decree Nisi will become a **Conditional Order**.
    - ✓ The Decree Absolute will become a **Final Divorce Order**.

- There will be a minimum period of **at least 20 weeks** that the Applicant/ Applicants must wait from the start of the proceedings, before applying for a Conditional Order. The 6-week period will stay between the Conditional Order and the Final Divorce Order.

- The changes will also impact Divorce, Dissolution (ending a Civil Partnership) and Judicial Separation.

It is likely many of the forms and procedures on divorce applications will change so important to watch this space!

CHAPTER 4

Problem scenarios

Problem questions and suggested answers

Problem question

A new client Sameera has come to see you regarding their marriage. She tells you she married Sayeed in 2010 in Croydon, London, and all the correct formalities for a marriage were followed. They have no children. She shows you her marriage certificate which you have checked. They moved into a house together in May 2010 where they have a joint mortgage. Sameera tells you that their relationship was great at first as they shared the same interests and enjoyed going out together for meals and events. However, Sayeed's behavior changed after they were married a couple of years. He started to say out late after work, refuses to help with any clearing up around the house, he has shouted and sworn at her when she asked him for some help and called her names. This treatment has continued. She admits to you that she felt neglected and unwanted by her husband and has been in a sexual relationship with another man, Mustafa. She is considering whether she wants to have a divorce of not and has not mentioned this to her husband Sayeed as yet. They remain living together in the same house but have separate rooms.

What is your advice to Sameera on her options?

Suggested answer

You should clarify if there was any evidence of domestic violence. In this scenario it appears not, which means that, Sameera is unlikely to be entitled to Legal Aid (she would also need to be of low means). Funding options to pay the legal fees/costs will need to be discussed with Sameera (fixed fees/pay-as-you-go/Sears Tooth agreement/loan etc). You should give general advice on divorce and any alternatives in particular mediation. Check marriage certificate and any other relevant documents.

It will not be your role to advise one way or the other on whether she should file for divorce. If you are a trainee solicitor for instance you are bound by professional codes of conduct on this. You will be advising objectively on options and process not guiding the client in any way. If Sameera decides to file for divorce you will advice her on the procedure as outlined in an earlier question on divorce procedure.

She first needs to know if she has any grounds for divorce. Sameera has told you that Sayeed's behaviour has changed towards her and appears to still be continuing. Under the <u>MCA 1973</u> The only ground for divorce under S.1(1) of the <u>MCA 1973</u> which that the marriage has `irretrievably broken down'. Sameera should be able to show there has been an irretrievable breakdown, based on one of the 5 facts (unreasonable behaviour). In this case S.1 (2) (b) of the <u>MCA 1973</u> states *"that the respondent has behaved in such a way that the petitioner cannot reasonably be expected to live with the respondent."*

The test for unreasonable behaviour was established by Mr Justice Dunn in the 1974 case *Livingstone-Stallard v Livingstone-Stallard [1974]* *"Would any right thinking person come to the conclusion that this husband has behaved in such a way that this wife cannot reasonably be expected to live with him, taking into account the whole of the circumstances and the character and personalities of the parties?"*

Any example of behaviour that left her feeling she could not remain married to the

Respondent (Sayeed) and where the most recent example took place within the six-month period that preceded her separation would usually be sufficient. She has been married to Sayeed for approximately 9 years so well beyond the minimum 1 year requirement. You can advise her if she meets this criteria she should be able to establish Sayeed's behaviour was unreasonable. Looking at the issue of her adultery based on her admission she had engaged in sexual intercourse outside of her marriage, this would not be relevant if she was the Petitioner, as her sexual would not constitute adultery.

Although it is only necessary to establish one of the 5 facts, it is worth considering the others and discarding them. Adultery has been dealt with. Desertion is not relevant as they still live together in the same house. Looking at two and five year separation facts these seem unlikely to be relevant (unless Sameera tells you otherwise) as both of them have continued to live together in the same household. Separation can potentially occur where the parties continue to live together but in separate rooms where they have both decided their marriage is over. In this scenario, there seems to be no information to show Sameera and Sayeed made a conscious decision to separate when they moved into separate rooms, more out of convenience *(Mouncer v Mouncer [1972])*.

You should advise Sameera she can cite unreasonable behaviour in her divorce Petition (Form D8), if that is the route she wishes to take, and advise her on procedures and timescales. If she wishes you to act for her you will need to draw up a draft petition which will need to be sent to the Respondent (Sayeed) which he/his lawyers can suggest changes. The complete procedure and documents to be sent and filed with the court are set out in questions and answer on divorce procedures in the previous chapter. There are no children involved so no orders required, but you should discuss financial matters concerning property and her legal rights.

Problem question

You are assisting a client Mary, with her divorce Petition. Mary tells you her husband John is a difficult and obstructive person. She is worried that he will not comply with the normal divorce procedure, and is unlikely to acknowledge service of any documents served on him. His address is known.

Can you advise Mary what are the best options available to her if he does not comply?

Suggested answer

There are some preferred options available to Mary in these circumstances. They are:-

- Personal service – Where there is no address for the Respondent. A statement of service needs to be filed. You have an address for Mary's husband's John, so this method is not appropriate. More relevant to advise using a Inquiry Agent or Process Server.

- Bailiff/Process Server – Need to try to get a signature and file a certificate and a fee is payable. Using a Bailiff would be cheaper but it will take longer to do. The advantage of using a Process Server is it will be quicker (but more expensive).

- Deemed service – Where the divorce Petition has been served on the respondent by post and you are satisfied they have received the Petition, you can ask the court to `deem service'. Thus despite the fact Harry may have not returned the Acknowledgment of Service, Mary can still apply for Decree Nisi. Evidence of text messages or emails that the Respondent has received the Petition can be relied on to support her application for deemed service. You will need supporting evidence such as a statement that will satisfy the District Judge that the papers were received.

Mary would be best advised to use one of the latter two options to serve the Petition and associated documents in the circumstances.

Problem question

Barbara comes to discuss her potential divorce suite against her husband. She has been married to her husband George for 7 years and they have two young children, twins Leah and Sophia aged 6. It had been a very equal partnership with George playing a full role as a father helping with the housework and looking after the children.

However, she tells you matters have changed and George has been staying out late at night more often in the last 12 months or so, and when she challenged him he became abusive towards her, shouting and screaming as well as throwing things on the floor, saying he could do what he wanted and it was none of her business. This left her upset as well as extremely tired being left with all the housework and getting the children fed and dressed and ready for school every morning without any help from George.

One day she was collecting clothes for washing and a piece of paper fell out of his pocket and she noticed a woman's name and phone number on it. Later that evening she challenged George over it and he confessed he had been seeing another woman in the evenings a couple of times a week and was having a sexual relationship with her.

She has moved out of the family home and has been staying with her sister along with their two children. She briefly returned to the family home for a few weeks after George begged her to return, but his pattern of behaviour was unchanged. She has been with her sister now for the last 6 months.

She has come to you to discuss divorcing George.

Suggested answer

You should discuss with Barbara any issues of domestic violence. In this situation it appears not, which means that she is unlikely to be entitled to Legal Aid (she would also need to be of low means). Funding options to pay the legal fees/costs will need to be discussed with Barbara (fixed fees/pay-as-you-go/Sears Tooth agreement/loan etc). You should give general advice on divorce and any alternatives in particular mediation. Check marriage certificate and any other relevant documents.

Barbara has been married for 7 years so meets the 1 year threshold (S.3(1) MCA 1973) and can petition for divorce immediately. She needs to establish that the marriage has broken down irretrievably (S.1(1) MCA 1973). Based on the facts she has given you, she should be able to demonstrate that the marriage had irretrievable broken down (S.1(1) MCA 1973). From the 5 facts clearly adultery and intolerability are present based on Georges sexual affair with another woman. Section 1(2)(a) MCA 1973 states *"that the respondent has committed adultery and the petitioner finds it intolerable to leave with the respondent"*. Adultery is voluntary sexual intercourse between a man and a woman, both of whom are married. Barbara has told you George has confessed to being in a sexual relationship which it is assumed has involved sexual intercourse (sexual intimacy that is short of sexual intercourse will not amount to adultery). To rely on adultery you need to show two things:-
- The respondent has committed adultery;

- The petitioner finds in intolerable to live with the respondent.

Barbara move out and apart from briefly returning home, she has lived away from George at her sisters for the last 6 months after finding out about his adultery, so passes this test (*Cleary v Cleary [1974]*[xiv]). Section 1(2)(b) MCA 1973 on behaviour may come into play. George has behaved in such a way that she cannot reasonably be expected to live with him (*Livingstone-Stallard v Livingstone Stallard [1974]* as discussed in previous question). She has not lived with him for 6 months since his admission of an affair and unreasonable behaviour shouting and screaming at her and throwing objects on the floor. In *Katz v Katz [1972]* [xv]it was stated that behaviour may be *"acts, omissions or a course of conduct"*. This fact would be relevant here for use in divorce petition. The other facts on 2-year and 5-year separation are not relevant, nor desertion.

You can use the facts and relevant law to start to draft the petition. As there are children involved the various orders she may need for provision on financial provision/maintenance orders etc for the children (as well as herself).

ABOUT THE AUTHOR

I have studied law for many years as a part time student and have both undergraduate and post graduate qualifications and have completed the LPC. I have worked in voluntary paralegal/legal support roles. I worked as a civil servant for many years dealing with health policy as well as well as employment and collective bargaining procedures and complex personal case work. I maintain a keen interest in legal issues in particular, as well as other areas of study. I currently work for a law firm specializing in employment law where I work as an advanced paralegal in legal practice and am a member of the Chartered Institute of Legal Executives.

[i] Hyde v Hyde [1886] LR 1 P&D 130
[ii] Bellinger v Bellinger [2001] HL 10
[iii] Corbett v Corbett [1970] 2 All ER 33
[iv] R v Jackson [1891] 1 QB 671, CA
[v] Reneville v de Reneville [1948] 1 All ER 56, CA
[vi] Pugh v Pugh [1951] 2 All E.R. 680
[vii] Gereis v Yacoub [1977] 1 FLR 854
[viii] Livingstone-Stallard v Livingstone-Stallard [1974] 2 All ER 766, [1974] Fam 47
[ix] https://www.gov.uk/apply-for-divorce
[x] https://brodies.com/sites/default/files/brexit_and_family_law.pdf

[xi] An example of how the Statement of Case may be included in the petition as drafted by a solicitor for instance could be:
Fact A - *In or about December 2018 in Smithwick, Dorchester the Respondent committed adultery with a person whom the Petitioner does not wish to name*
Fact D – *The parties separated on 5 January 2017 and have not lived together since that time.*

[xii] The Family Law and Practice CLP Legal Practice Guide (Duffield N, Kempton J, Sabine C – Family Law and Practice 2017 / College of Law Publishing 2017) makes the point that the petitioner could also be prejudiced as orders for periodical payments can only be backdated to the date of the application, which will be the date of the petition, unless leave of the court is needed for a later application when it will be the date of the actual application. Also, where a petitioner remarries, he will then be prevented from making a claim for a lump sum or property adjustment order. If on the other hand he had applied in the prayer (that is before the remarriage), a hearing could have taken place after he/she remarried. Financial orders can be claimed on the standard form for any children of the family in the form of lump sum orders, but the Child Maintenance Service (CMS) tend to deal with periodical payments.

[xiii] UKSC 41
[xiv] Cleary v Cleary [1974] 1 WLR 73 (CA)
[xv] Katz v Katz [1972] I W.L.R. 955;. 3 All E.R. 219

www.ingramcontent.com/pod-product-compliance
Lightning Source LLC
Chambersburg PA
CBHW040231220526
45473CB00001B/204